U.S. Fish & Wildlife Service

Molt and Aging Criteria for Four North American Grassland Passerines

Biological Technical Publication

BTP-R6011-2008

Peter Pyle[1]

Stephanie L. Jones[2]

Janet M. Ruth[3]

[1] The Institute for Bird Populations, Point Reyes Station, CA
[2] U.S. Fish and Wildlife Service, Nongame Migratory Bird Program Region 6, Denver, CO
[3] U.S. Geological Survey, Arid Lands Field Station, Albuquerque, NM

Author contact information:
Peter Pyle
The Institute for Bird Populations
P.O. Box 1346
Point Reyes Station, CA 94956
Phone: (415) 663-2053
E-mail: ppyle@birdpop.org

Stephanie L. Jones
U.S. Fish and Wildlife Service
Region 6 Nongame Migratory Bird Coordinator
P.O. Box 25486 DFC
Denver, CO 80225
Phone: (303) 236-4409
E-mail: stephanie_jones@fws.gov

Janet M. Ruth
Research Ecologist
U.S. Geological Survey
Fort Collins Science Center
Arid Lands Field Station
Biology Department MSC03 2020
1 University of New Mexico
Albuquerque, NM 87131-0001
Phone: (505) 346-2870
E-mail: janet_ruth@usgs.gov

For additional copies or information, contact:
U.S. Fish and Wildlife Service
Region 6 Nongame Migratory Bird Coordinator
P.O. Box 25486 DFC
Denver, CO 80225

Recommended citation:
Pyle, P., S.L. Jones, and J. M. Ruth. 2008. Molt and aging criteria for four North American grassland passerines. U.S. Department of Interior, Fish and Wildlife Service, Biological Technical Publication, FWS/BTP-R6011-2008, Washington, D.C.

Table of Contents

List of Figures

Acknowledgments

This document resulted from a U.S. Fish and Wildlife Service, Migratory Bird Office Region 6, grant to the Institute for Bird Populations (IBP) for the study of molt. We thank Stephen K. Davis for sharing images of Sprague's Pipits at a workshop in Saskatoon, Saskatchewan, Canada, and David DeSante (IBP) for support and help administering the contract. We also thank Steve N.G. Howell for use of illustrations (Figures 2-6) from Pyle (1997a) and Maureen Flannery at the California Academy of Science and Carla Cicero at Museum of Vertebrate Zoology for allowing examination of specimens. We thank Michael T. Green, Kevin Kritz, and Maiken Winter for providing helpful comments on earlier drafts of this manuscript. This is contribution number 303 of the Institute for Bird Populations.

Introduction

Prairie and grassland habitats in central and western North America have declined substantially since settlement by Europeans (Knopf 1994) and many of the birds and other organisms that inhabit North American grasslands have experienced steep declines (Peterjohn and Sauer 1999; Johnson and Igl 1997; Sauer, Hines, and Fallon 2007). The species addressed here, Sprague's Pipit (*Anthus spragueii*), Grasshopper (*Ammodramus savannarum*) and Baird's (*A. bairdii*) sparrows, and Chestnut-collared Longspurs (*Calcarius ornatus*), are grassland birds that are of special conservation concern throughout their ranges due to declining populations and the loss of the specific grassland habitats required on both their breeding and wintering ranges (Knopf 1994, Davis and Sealy 1998, Davis 2003, Davis 2004, Jones and Dieni 2007).

Population-trend data on grassland birds, while clearly showing declines, provides no information on the causes of population declines. Without demographic information (i.e., productivity and survivorship), there are no means to determine when in their life cycle the problems that are creating these declines are occurring, or to determine to what extent population trends are driven by factors that affect birth rates, death rates, or both (DeSante 1995). For migratory birds, population declines may be driven by factors on breeding grounds, during migration, and/or on wintering grounds. Lack of data on productivity and survivorship thus impedes the formulation of effective management and conservation strategies to reverse population declines (DeSante 1992). Furthermore, if deficiencies in survivorship are revealed, management strategies may need to address habitats on both breeding and non-breeding grounds, as well as along migratory pathways. One technique that helps inform management strategies is the biochemical analysis of isotopes and genetic markers, from the sampling of individual feathers from live birds (Smith et al. 2003, Pérez and Hobson 2006; Appendix).

Determining demographic parameters and effectively sampling feathers to reveal connectivity between breeding and wintering grounds requires detailed knowledge of molt patterns and age determination criteria for the target species, in the hand. For example, productivity, survivorship, and territory acquisition may all be age-dependent, with first-year birds showing different patterns and responses than older birds. In many cases it may be possible to sample both a feather grown on the breeding grounds and one grown on the wintering grounds from a single individual, but knowledge of age-specific molt patterns, as well as an ability to recognize different feather generations, is needed to accomplish such a task. While some information on molt and aging criteria exists for grassland passerine species (Pyle 1997a), these species have been rarely captured during mark-recapture studies (Jones et al. 2007) and this information thus needs refining. There is a need for additional resources to assist field workers in determining molt patterns and age in captured individuals.

Our objective is to describe molt and aging criteria for four grassland passerine species with the aid of digital photographs taken in the field. We hope that this document will be useful for researchers studying grassland species through capture and banding of live individuals on either the breeding or the wintering grounds. We present a general section on molt and aging techniques, followed by specific accounts for the four species treated: Sprague's Pipits, Grasshopper and Baird sparrows, and Chestnut-collared Longspur. We also provide a brief protocol on collecting feather samples (Appendix).

Molt and Aging by Molt Limits

Molt and plumage terminology used here follow Humphrey and Parkes (1959) as modified by Howell et al. (2003), and age terminology follows the calendar-based system presented by Pyle (1997a).

Preformative and prebasic molts.--Passerines typically undergo a preformative molt (referred to as "first prebasic molt" in Pyle 1997a) in their first summer and fall, and a complete prebasic molt in July to October following breeding (Figure 1). For migratory species these molts can occur on the breeding grounds, on molting grounds away from breeding or wintering grounds, or on the wintering grounds; or, they can begin on breeding or molting grounds, suspend for migration, and complete on wintering grounds (Pyle 1997a). Which of these strategies is undertaken can vary both among species and among individuals of the same species (Figure 1). In Sprague's Pipits, the location(s) where the preformative and prebasic molts occur have yet to be determined.

The preformative molt undergone by first-cycle, hatching year/second year (hereafter "HY/SY"), passerines in July through September (Howell et al. 2003; Figure 1) shows substantial inter- and intra-specific variation in both extent (varying from partial

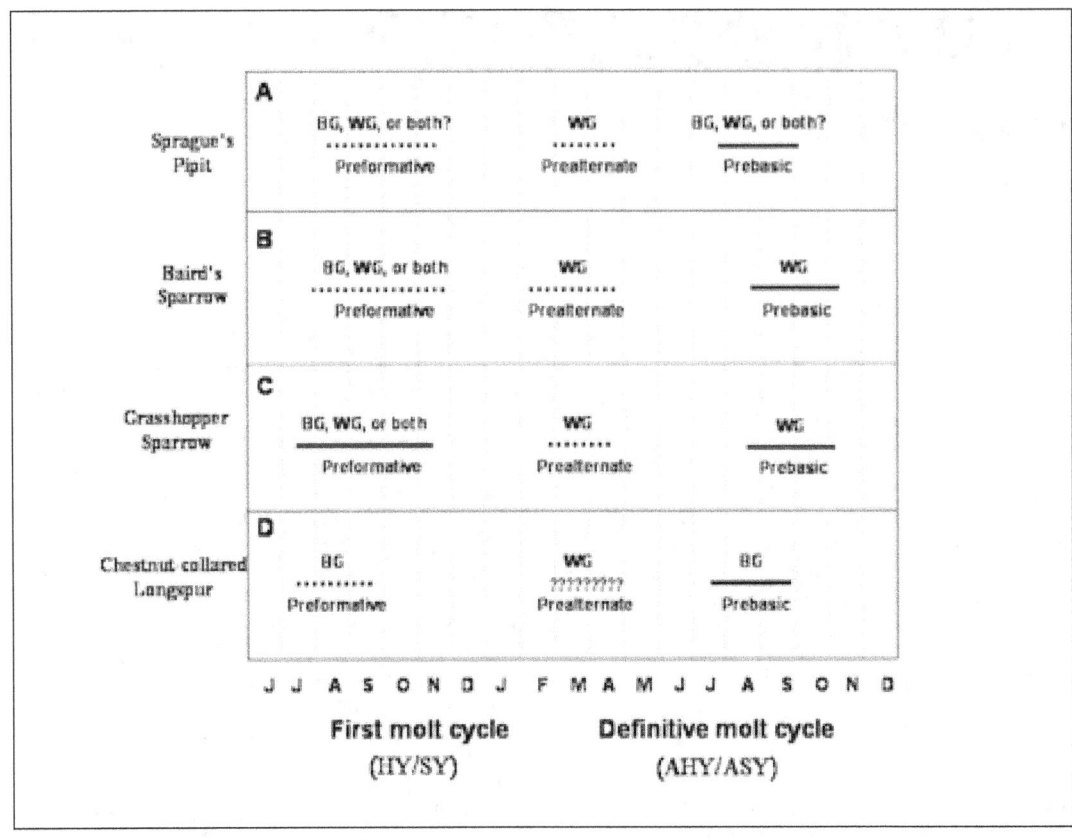

Figure 1. Molt patterns among four species of grassland passerines during the first and definitive molt cycles. Solid bars indicate complete molts and dashed bars indicate incomplete, limited, or partial molts. Locations of where molts occur are indicated above the bars: BG = breeding grounds; WG = wintering grounds.

to complete) and in location of occurrence (Pyle 1997a). In some species (including Grasshopper Sparrows) the preformative molt is typically complete, and thereafter it becomes difficult or impossible to separate HY/SY from older after hatching year/after second year (hereafter "AHY/ASY") individuals by plumage-related criteria. In most passerine species; however, this molt is partial or incomplete. HY/SYs can be separated from AHY/ASYs throughout the year by the presence of "molt limits" (see below for details) within feather tracts (Figure 2; Pyle 1997a, 1997b; Froehlich 2003), particularly those of the wing (Figure 2), and sometimes among the rectrices (tail feathers). Some passerines, particularly those that inhabit sunny or harsh environments, can also replace outer primaries during what is known as an eccentric preformative molt (Pyle 1997a, 1997b; see Figure 6). Although undocumented in the four species treated here, it appears that at least some Sprague's Pipits may undergo such a molt (see species account below).

Prealternate molt.-- Prealternate molts typically occur before spring migration on wintering grounds (February to April). All four species treated here are reported to have limited or partial prealternate molts (Figure 1; but see the Grasshopper Sparrow

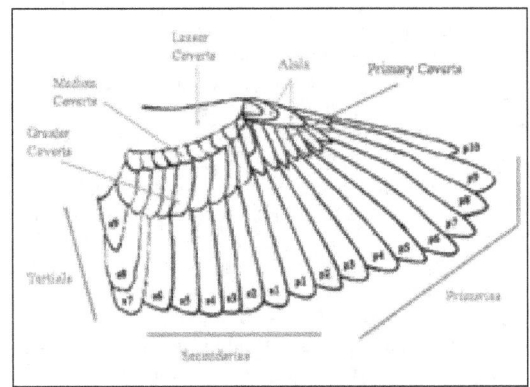

Figure 2. Tracts of the wing for identification of molt limits in grassland passerines. The primary covert tract is emphasized because it is often the best tract to use to separate SYs from ASYs in spring. Primaries are numbered distally and secondaries are numbered proximally, reflecting the order in which they molt (except for the tertials, which molt before other secondaries). Note that the "tertials" are usually considered a subset of the secondaries, s7-s9. Illustration: Steve N.G. Howell

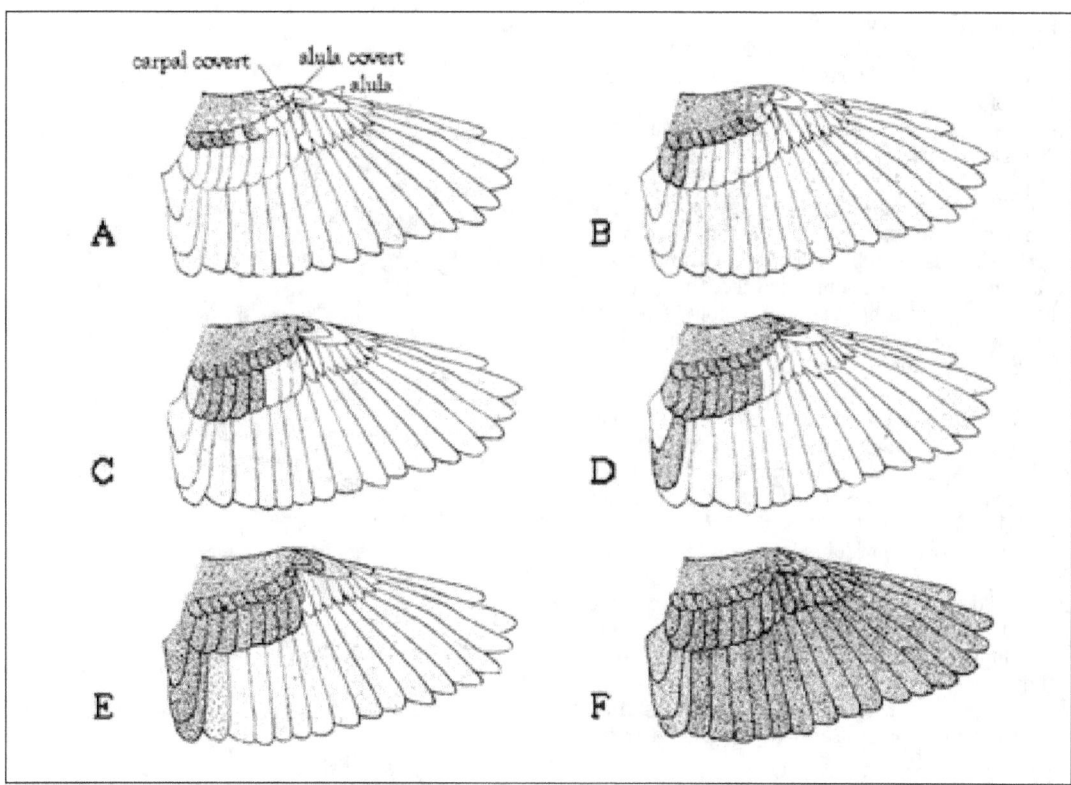

Figure 3. Indication of molt limits within the wings of grassland passerines. Darker feathers indicate those replaced during the preformative (or prealternate) molt. **A-E** indicate limits resulting from varying extents of these molts. **F** represents uniform feather tracts following a complete molt. Illustration: Steve N.G. Howell.

and Chestnut-collared Longspur accounts). This can result in up to two generations of feathers (basic and alternate) in ASYs and up to three generations (juvenal, formative, and alternate) in SYs (see Sprague's Pipits and Grasshopper Sparrows species accounts, below). Alternate feathers are typically worn only for three to five months and can be poorly constructed and "looser", as in juvenal feathers. In grassland species, these alternate feathers also typically occur in more exposed areas, such as among scapulars, inner and/or central wing coverts, tertials, and central rectrices. The prealternate molt is seldom more complete than the preformative molt. The use of molt limits, as in fall and winter birds (Figures 3 and 4), continues to be a reliable method of aging, once alternate feathers are recognized (Figure 5). The recognition of alternate feathers is also a crucial step in determining which feathers to sample for connectivity studies.

Molt limits.-- Molt limits are visual differences in feather color, shape, amount of wear, and quality within and between feather tracts due to differing feather generations resulting from partial molts. Molt limits occur most frequently and are easiest to identify among feather tracts of the wing. In October-March, HY/SYs of species that have incomplete preformative molts will show molt limits among the lesser, median, and greater coverts

(Figure 3**A-D**); between the secondary coverts and the primary coverts (Figures 3**E** and 4); and/or among the tertials and inner secondaries (Figure 3**D-E**). Some individuals, particularly those with more extensive wing molts (Figure 3**D-E**), may also replace the two central rectrices. Replaced feathers are formative whereas retained feathers, including most or all primaries, secondaries, and rectrices, are juvenal feathers developed at the natal site. Thus, through February on the wintering grounds, look for molt limits in the patterns of Figures 3**A-E**, 4, and 5 on HY/SYs, and look for uniform basic feathers as in Figure 3**F** on HY/SY Grasshopper Sparrows and AHY/ASYs of all four species treated here.

Juvenal feathers are typically of poorer quality than formative or basic feathers, and because of this are increasingly (through time) affected by feather wear. This is especially true of grassland species, where feathers of the upperparts and wing are typically exposed to more sunlight and abrading vegetation than woodland species. Juvenal wing coverts and tertials can often be recognized by their paler coloration and frayed tips, especially when in direct contrast with formative feathers (Froehlich 2003). Juvenal flight feathers, particularly the outer primaries and rectrices, can wear more rapidly, resulting in a thinner shape and more frayed tips, especially in the spring and early summer. In

Sprague's Pipits, Baird's Sparrows, and Chestnut-collared Longspurs, the presence of contrasts between juvenal and formative feathers, and the shape of the outer primaries and rectrices, are useful means of aging birds in winter and early spring (Pyle 1997a, 1997b).

The ability to recognize feather generations on breeding and wintering birds is essential both for accurate aging of birds in the hand, and for assessing where in the annual cycle (e.g., on the breeding or wintering grounds) sampled feathers were developed using stable isotopes (Appendix; see Pérez and Hobson 2006) or other means.

The following species accounts give details of molt and aging, accompanied by digital images, of each of the four species treated in this report. Live individuals of the four species were photographed by SLJ and JMR in 2004-2006 during a long-term banding study at Bowdoin National Wildlife Refuge in Phillips Co., north-central Montana (Dieni and Jones 2003, Jones et al. 2007). Individuals were lured into 30 or 36-mm mesh mist nets using tape playback recordings of conspecific song (Jones et al. 2007). Study skins housed at the California Academy of Sciences, San Francisco, California, and the Museum of Vertebrate Zoology, Berkeley, California, were examined by PP.

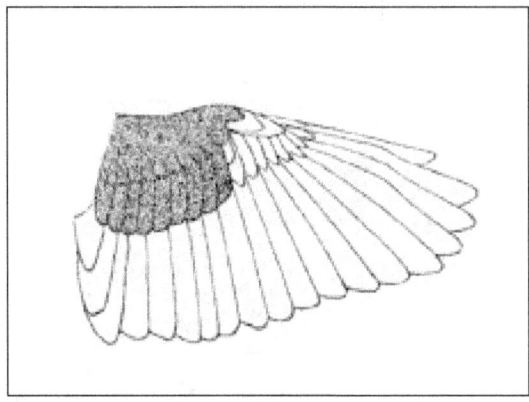

Figure 4. A common molt-limit pattern found in certain SY passerines, including Baird's Sparrows. Darker feathers are formative and paler feathers are juvenal. Illustration: Steve N.G. Howell

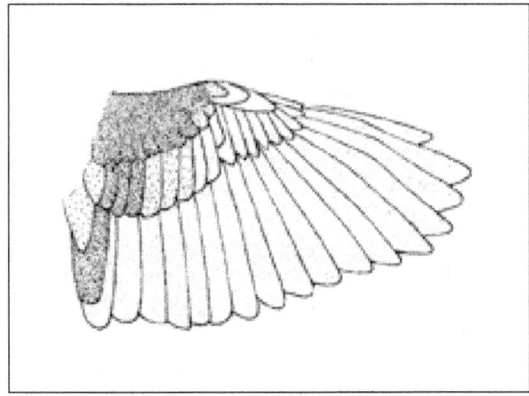

Figure 5. Juvenal (white), formative (stippled), and alternate (dark) feathers following the first-prealternate molt in certain passerines. Illustration: Steve N.G. Howell

Figure 6. Eccentric molt pattern among the primaries and secondaries. Note the replaced formative outer primaries and inner secondaries contrasting with a block of juvenal feathers in the center of the wing. Sprague's Pipits may show this pattern. Illustration: Steve N.G. Howell

Species Accounts

Baird's Sparrow.

SPRAGUE'S PIPIT (*Anthus spragueii*)

Molt.--Our knowledge of molts in this species is rudimentary, based almost entirely on examination of a small ($n = 15$) number of specimens (Pyle 1997a, 1997b). Thus, banding and feather-sampling studies will continue to be extremely useful in confirming, updating, or correcting available information. In HYs (hatching year), the preformative molt reportedly occurs from August-October and is partial to incomplete (Figure 1A). Where this molt occurs (on the breeding, molting, or wintering grounds) in Sprague's Pipits is unknown; isotopic analysis (Appendix) would be useful in determining this (see below).

The preformative molt typically includes most or all body feathers, 5-10 greater coverts, and usually (in 80%; $n = 15$) 1-4 tertials/inner secondaries (Pyle 1997a, 1997b). For HY/SYs in formative plumage (September-March), molt limits will occur among the median and greater coverts, between the greater and primary coverts, and/or among the tertials (Figures 3B-E, 7, and 8). No rectrices are reported to be replaced during the preformative molt but study is needed to confirm this (see below).

It appears that at least three SY individuals captured in Montana in June 2006 may have undergone eccentric preformative molts, replacing four outer primaries and the tertials (Figure 8). Species that undergo eccentric preformative primary molts typically also replace all rectrices and at least two of these individuals appeared to have had done so (see below). Another possibility, however, may be that birds showing this pattern are ASYs that had suspended molt for migration after replacing the inner five primaries, but it seems more likely that this was an eccentric molt on an SY, as found in many other passerines (Pyle 1997b).

Eccentric molts have not been previously reported for Sprague's Pipits but could occur based on the species' exposed habitat preferences, where feathers degrade quickly from bleaching and/or abrasion (Pyle 1997a). Lark Bunting (*Calamospiza melanocorys*), a species with similar migration patterns and habitat requirements, also has an eccentric molt pattern (2-5 outer primaries replaced) and renews all rectrices during the preformative molt (Pyle 1997a) so it might not be an unexpected pattern in the unstudied Sprague's Pipit.

In AHYs, the prebasic molt occurs from August-September and is complete (Figure 1A). As with the preformative molt, the location where this molt occurs has yet to be determined. Because this molt is complete, AHY/ASYs in basic plumage (September-March) will not show molt limits (Figure 3F), although it is possible that a suspension of molt for migration may simulate a molt limit (see Figure 8).

The first and subsequent prealternate molts are limited to partial, and occur in March and April on the wintering grounds (Figure 1A). The first prealternate molt in SYs usually (75%; $n = 15$) includes 1-3 inner greater coverts, 1-3 tertials, and sometimes (25%; $n = 15$) 1-2 central rectrices (Pyle 1997b). In the wing it is less extensive than the preformative molt so, by ignoring alternate feathers, molt limits between juvenal and formative feathers will still be useful in identifying SYs in April through August (Figure 5). In ASYs the prealternate molt may average more extensive, including 3-5 inner or medial greater coverts, 2-3 tertials, and (more often than in SYs) 1-2 central rectrices. Thus, ASYs in March-August may show molt limits resembling Figure 3C-D, but with 2-3 tertials replaced.

Age Determination.--In September-March, HY/SY Sprague's Pipits will show molt limits among the greater coverts and/or tertials (Figures 3B-E). Replaced formative coverts will be noticeably darker and fresher looking than retained juvenal coverts (Figures 7, 8, and 9). It appears that some SYs may also have replaced the outer primaries in eccentric sequence during their preformative molt (Figure 6) and thus show molt limits between the outer and inner primaries (Figures 8 and 9). It is probable that these primaries may not have been replaced until October and November on the wintering grounds but more study is needed to determine this. AHY/ASYs in September-March, by contrast, should show uniformly basic secondary coverts and tertials (Figure 3F). The greater coverts may contrast slightly in color with the primary coverts but these feather tracts will appear uniform in feather quality (see Baird's Sparrows species account below). On HY/SYs, the primary coverts are juvenal feathers and will appear tapered and worn as compared with the broader, less worn basic primary coverts of AHY/ASYs (Figure 7). In addition, juvenal rectrices will be narrower and more pointed in HY/SYs than in AHY/ASYs (Figure 10); however, individuals with adult-like rectrices should be checked carefully for eccentric molt patterns (Figure 8). These individuals may replace all rectrices with formative feathers that resemble basic feathers (Figure 11).

In spring (February-June), both SYs and ASYs may show molt limits resulting from prealternate molts, but some formative feathers usually remain on SYs, allowing the continued use of molt limits to age these (Figures 5, 7, 9, 11, and 12). Eccentric molt patterns among the primaries would continue to indicate SY (Figures 6 and 8). Otherwise, the shape and the condition of the primary coverts (Figure 7) may be the best method of separating SYs from ASYs. Some individuals may also retain juvenal rectrices (Figures 10 and 12) which would be of continued use in aging; however, individuals with adult-like rectrices may be SYs that had replaced them during the preformative molt (see Figure 11) and, thus, ASYs should not be aged by rectrix shape alone.

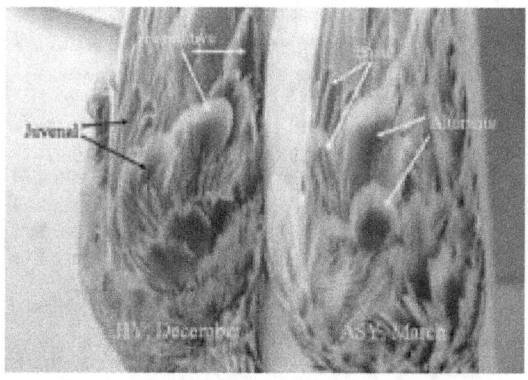

Figure 7. Specimens of HY and ASY Sprague's Pipit (collected in Texas) demonstrating molt limits between formative and juvenal feathers (HY) and alternate and basic feathers (ASY). Note that the juvenal primary coverts on HYs are more tapered and worn than the basic primary coverts on ASYs. The difference becomes more obvious when comparing SYs with ASYs in spring. Photo: Peter Pyle

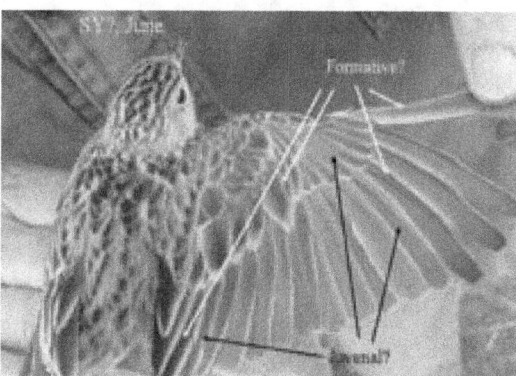

Figure 8. Apparent SY Sprague's Pipit (from Montana) showing eccentric preformative molt patterns. Note that the outer four primaries appear fresher, darker, and with darker shafts than the inner five primaries. The three tertials also appear to have been replaced during the preformative and/or prealternate molts, as would be typical in individuals replacing the outer four primaries. The left wing showed the same patterns of replacement. Based on images of the tail, it is difficult to determine whether or not the rectrices were replaced during the preformative molt. Photo: Janet M. Ruth

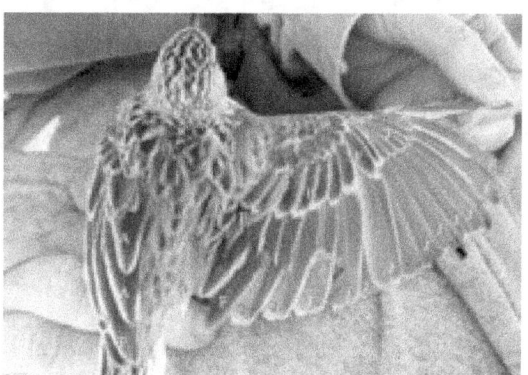

Figure 9. Feather generations among wing feathers in an apparent SY Sprague's Pipit, captured in Montana in June. J = juvenal, F = formative, and A = alternate feather; red indicates good feathers to sample for connectivity studies. Photo: Janet M. Ruth

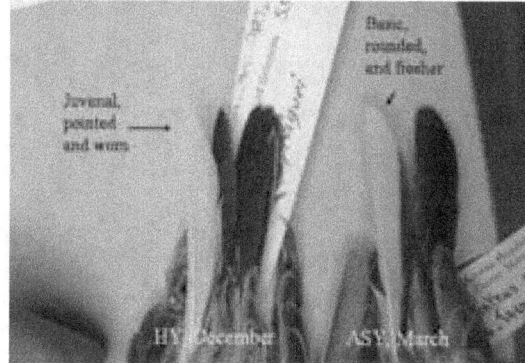

Figure 10. Rectrix shape and condition by age in Sprague's Pipit specimens (collected in Texas). Note that by spring the juvenal outer rectrix shown above will become even more worn and frayed in comparison to the basic outer rectrix. Juvenal rectrices might be replaced during the preformative molt but at what frequency is unknown (see Figures 11 and 12). Photo: Peter Pyle

Feather Sampling for Biochemical Analysis.--As alluded to above, much can still be learned about molt in Sprague's Pipits based on biochemical analysis. At any time of year, juvenal feathers can be recognized in the wing (and at least sometimes the rectrices) and sampled to determine the location or latitude of the natal site. Perhaps the best strategy would be to sample some barbs from the base of the innermost primary, which will always be a juvenal feather on SYs. For ASYs this feather should indicate where the prebasic molt commenced, either on the breeding grounds, the wintering grounds, or perhaps at a molting stopover site. On HY/SYs showing eccentric patterns it would also be useful to sample barbs from the first replaced primary (e.g., p6 in the individuals in Figures 8 and 9). This should indicate where this eccentric portion of the preformative molt occurred, most likely on the wintering grounds or at a stopover location. Sampling of both an inner and an outer primary in ASYs could also reveal whether or not the prebasic molt was suspended for migration (Pérez and Hobson 2006).

In spring, look also for different generations of wing coverts (e.g., Figure 5; the ASY in Figure 7) and tertials on both SYs and ASYs. It would probably be easiest to sample from tertials and inner secondaries, as varying numbers of tertials are usually replaced during preformative and prealternate molts (Figures 8 and 9), and in some individuals up to two or even three generations of feathers may be present in these tracts. In Figure 9, for example, signals from the natal site (s1-s5), the location of the preformative molt (s6, s7 and s9), and the location of the prealternate molt (s8) might all be detected by taking barb samples from secondaries of the right wing. On ASYs, the locations of both the prebasic and the prealternate molts may similarly be detected by sampling basic and alternate feathers among the tertials. Signals from two to three locations might also be detected by taking a sample from a central rectrix (often replaced during the prealternate molt) along with samples from one or more other, more distal rectrices (Figure 12).

We recommend taking samples from several feathers among the primaries, greater coverts, secondaries, tertials, and rectrices, to gain a better understanding of how extensive each molt is and where it occurs. Even within tracts, it is possible that different feathers have been replaced at different locations within the same molt. We would recommend taking samples from p1 (Figure 2) and an outer primary in fall and winter, as well as from the greater coverts and/or inner secondaries and tertials in spring.

Figures 11 & 12. Rectrices in two apparent SY Sprague's Pipits captured for banding in Montana in June. Both of these individuals showed apparent eccentric patterns in the wings. Many passerines with eccentric patterns replace all rectrices during the preformative molt but more study is needed (e.g., through biochemical analysis) to determine rectrix-replacement patterns in this species. Photos: Janet M. Ruth

Grasshopper Sparrow.

GRASSHOPPER SPARROW (*Ammodramus savannarum*)

Molt.--In HY Grasshopper Sparrows, the preformative molt occurs from July to November and is usually complete (Figure 1C). Pyle (1997a) indicates that occasional HY/SYs may retain some medial juvenal secondaries during the preformative molt but this appears to be a rare occurrence. This molt can take place on the breeding grounds, wintering grounds, or both, being suspended for migration. As in Baird's Sparrows (see below), the tertials and inner greater coverts are naturally blacker, representing "pseudolimits" (Pyle 1997a: 207-208; Figure 13). Thus, although it may appear that there are molt limits, most to all HY/SYs should have uniformly formative feathers following the preformative molt.

In AHY Grasshopper Sparrows, the prebasic molt occurs from July - September and is complete (Figure 1C). It reportedly occurs primarily on the breeding grounds but this should be confirmed with biochemical analysis. Grasshopper Sparrows may undergo unusual breeding and migration strategies, and some birds (at least) may show variable molt patterns with relation to migration (Vickery 1996). Because this molt is complete, AHY/ASYs in basic plumage (September to March) will not show molt limits (Figure 3F), and will thus be similar in appearance to HY/SYs (Figure 13). However, occasional HY/SYs (perhaps 20-30%, $n = 40$) may retain juvenal secondaries among s4-s6 during the preformative molt (Pyle 1997a; Figure 14). Pyle (1997a) also reports that some birds may undergo a prealternate molt of some body feathers but this report also needs to be confirmed, perhaps through biochemical analysis. Such a limited prealternate molt might include feathers of the head and upper back (Figures 13 and 15).

Age Determination.--Because both the preformative and the prebasic molts are complete in most Grasshopper Sparrows it is not possible to age most individuals to HY/SY once the skulls undergo complete ossification in October through February, although those HY/SYs that retain secondaries among s4-s6 may be recognized to age by molt limits within this tract (see Figure 14). Another area to look for retained juvenal feathers in Grasshopper Sparrows is among the underwing coverts. For example, during the preformative molt many blackbirds replace all feathers except for the primary and some greater coverts on the underwing (Pyle 1997a) and it is possible that other species may show this feather-retention pattern as well. Look for paler and more worn juvenal underwing coverts contrasting with darker and more glossy replaced coverts (see Figure 323 in Pyle 1997a).

In some species, formative feathers can show retained characteristics of juvenal plumage. For a species like Grasshopper Sparrows, which can have a complete preformative molt, it would be useful to document what juvenal feathers look like on juvenile birds in summer and early fall, and to see if formative-plumaged birds in winter and spring may retain some of these juvenal characteristics. Otherwise, biochemical analysis might provide clues to aging, since the preformative molt can occur on the wintering grounds and the prebasic molt is supposed to occur on the breeding grounds (see below).

Feather Sampling for Biochemical Analysis.--It is likely that more can be learned about molt and aging of Grasshopper Sparrows through biochemical analysis than for any of the other three species covered in this report. It is known that some HYs migrate in juvenal or partial juvenal plumage, indicating that some feathers can be replaced on the wintering grounds or on molting grounds (Pyle 1997a). Thus, samples from p1, p9, the tertials (s7-s9), and s6 will help us determine where these feathers were replaced. Likewise, the outer and central rectrices might be good feathers to sample. If any feathers appear to have been replaced adventitiously (e.g., Figure 16), it would be good to compare them with adjacent feathers that have not been replaced. Finally, search for newer-looking feathers among the scapulars and/or in the back (Figures 13 and 15) that might represent alternate feathers. Sampling these (along with adjacent, more worn feathers) would not only help confirm the presence and extent of a prealternate molt, it might also help determine both wintering and molting grounds for the same individual.

Figure 13. Grasshopper Sparrow captured for banding in Montana. Note that all wing feathers appear to be uniform in quality, part of a single generation of either formative or basic feathers. The darker tertials and proximal greater coverts represent pseudolimits rather than replaced feathers of a newer generation. Some of the scapulars may represent alternate feathers. Photo: Janet M. Ruth

Figure 14. Grasshopper Sparrow captured for banding in Montana in June. Note the more worn secondaries (especially s2-s6) perhaps representing retained juvenal feathers. Photo: Janet M. Ruth

Figure 15. Grasshopper Sparrow captured for banding in Montana in June. Look for darker and fresher feathers among the back and scapulars that could represent alternate feathers replaced on the wintering grounds. It would be of interest to compare the biochemical signals from these feathers with those of older, adjacent feathers. Photo: Janet M. Ruth

Figure 16. Rectrices of a Grasshopper Sparrow captured for banding in Montana in June. The central rectrices were likely replaced due to accident rather than molt. It would be of interest to sample one of these, along with one of the other rectrices, to compare locations of development. Photo: Janet M. Ruth

BAIRD'S SPARROW (*Ammodramus bairdii*)

Molt.--In HY Baird's Sparrows, the preformative molt occurs from July - November and is partial (Figure 1**B**). According to the literature (e.g., Pyle 1997a) this molt can take place on the breeding grounds, the wintering grounds, or both, being suspended for migration. The preformative molt typically includes most or all contour feathers and all secondary coverts but no primary coverts, primaries, or secondaries. Thus, molt limits (Figure 4) result from the preformative molt. Pyle (1997a, 1997b) reports that 2-3 tertials are also typically replaced during the preformative molt, but this should be confirmed based on biochemical analysis. The tertials (and inner greater coverts) are naturally blacker in this species, resulting in "pseudolimits" (Figures 18 and 19; Pyle 1997a: 207-208), and thus, it can be difficult to assess whether or not these feathers had been replaced during preformative and/or prealternate molts. The central rectrices are also replaced often during the preformative molt (Figure 20). In AHYs the prebasic molt occurs from August - November and is complete (Figure 1**B**). It reportedly occurs primarily on the wintering grounds but this should also be confirmed with biochemical analysis. Because this molt is complete, AHY/ASYs in basic plumage (September-March) will not show molt limits (Figure 3**F**).

The first and subsequent prealternate molts in Baird's Sparrows are partial, and occur in February-April on the wintering grounds (Figure 1**B**). Although molt limits among the greater coverts will occur in about half of birds in spring, the limit between the formative outer greater coverts and juvenal primary coverts will be present in all SYs (Figures 17 and 18).The first and subsequent prealternate molts are similar in extent sometimes including 1-5 inner greater coverts and 1-3 tertials (30-50% of individuals), and occasionally including 1-2 central rectrices (~17% of individuals; $n = 26$). When no wing feathers are renewed, scapulars adjacent to the wing often have been replaced and can be recognized as fresher feathers (Figures 18 and 19). ASYs will have no limit in this area (Figure 19).

Age Determination.--The best way to age Baird's Sparrows throughout the year is by the presence or absence of a molt limit between the greater coverts and the primary coverts (Figures 4, 17 and 18). Juvenal primary coverts in HY/SYs, especially toward the outer portion of the wing, are typically frayed, narrow, and pale brown. These contrast with the darker and fresher, replaced, formative greater coverts (Figures 17 and 18). In AHY/ASYs the primary coverts are darker, broader and fresher (Figures 17 and 19) and do not contrast in quality with the greater coverts (Figure 19). This difference is not affected by the prealternate molt and is thus valid for aging Baird's Sparrows throughout the year.

Other useful criteria include the shape and condition of the primaries (Figures 18 and 19) and the rectrices (Figures 20 and 21). By using a combination of all of these criteria it will be possible to age most or all birds encountered on the breeding grounds.

Feather Sampling for Biochemical Analysis.--As with Sprague's Pipits, it should be possible to obtain feather samples representing breeding, molting, and wintering sites from Baird's Sparrows, often from the same individual. On HY/SYs in both winter and summer, feathers developed on the breeding site include the primaries, secondaries, and outer rectrices, possibly excepting the tertials in a few individuals. As the preformative molt can occur on breeding grounds, wintering grounds, or both, it will be of interest to sample multiple formative feathers, to try and establish the locations of both of these grounds and perhaps additional molting areas. Feathers molted earlier in the preformative molt include those of the crown and upper back, whereas later molted feathers include the scapulars, tertials (if replaced), and central rectrices (if replaced). The wing coverts are typically replaced all at once, and it would be interesting to know where this occurred, so taking a formative greater covert (toward the outside of the tract) would also be of value. On AHY/ASYs sampled on the wintering grounds, all feathers may produce winter-ground signals but it would be interesting to see if some birds may begin the prebasic molt on the breeding grounds, and this might be established by taking a sample from the innermost primary, or feathers of the crown and back. In addition, it is possible (but unlikely for this species) that birds may interrupt migration to molt somewhere north of the wintering grounds, in which case these or other feather samples may provide this information. In spring, winter signals should be obtained from alternate feathers among greater coverts (Figure 17 and 22), tertials (Figure 22), scapulars (Figures 18, 19, and 22), and central rectrices (Figures 20 and 21).

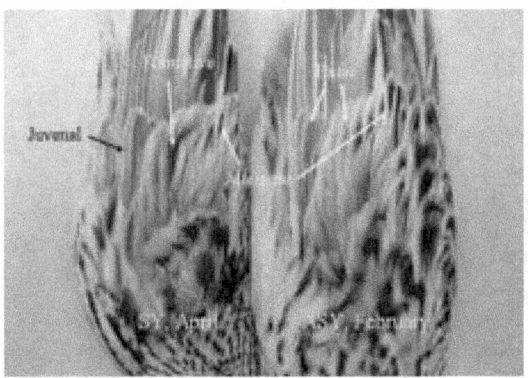

Figure 17. Specimens of SY and ASY Baird's Sparrows (collected in Arizona) demonstrating the molt limit between the formative greater coverts and juvenal primary coverts in the SY, lacking in the ASY. Note the difference in quality of the primary coverts, and that both individuals had replaced 2-3 inner greater coverts during the prealternate molt. Photo: Peter Pyle

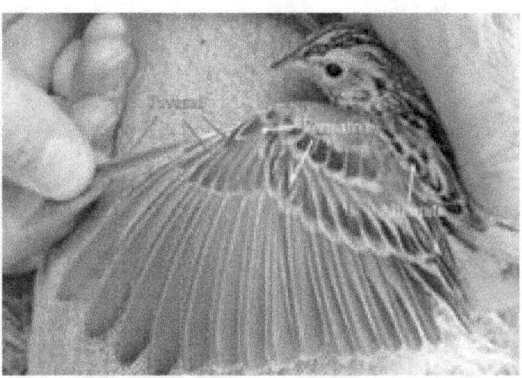

Figure 18. SY Baird's Sparrow in Montana in June showing molt limits in the wing. Note that the replaced formative greater coverts appear fresher and of better quality than the retained juvenal primary coverts (compare with Figure 19). Note also that the lesser alula appears to be replaced formative whereas the greater alula appears to be retained juvenal. Due to possible pseudolimits among tertials, it is difficult to tell whether or not they were replaced at the preformative molt. The juvenal outer primary is also narrow at the tip. This individual appears not to have replaced any tertials or greater coverts during the prealternate molt (the darker inner coverts resulting from pseudolimits) but appears to have newer alternate scapulars that can be used for feather sampling. Photo: Janet M. Ruth

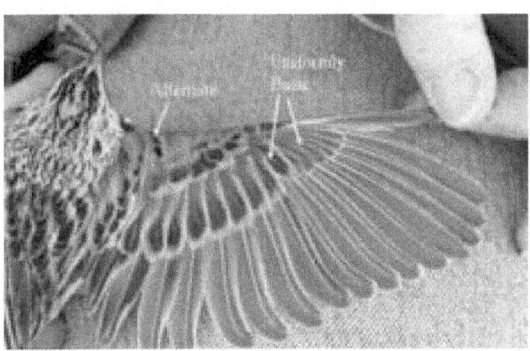

Figure 19. ASY Baird's Sparrow in Montana in June showing uniformly basic feathers in the wing. In contrast to the SY in Figure 18, note the darker and higher-quality primary coverts, not contrasting as markedly with the greater coverts, which are slightly darker in color (naturally) than the primary coverts but uniform in wear and quality. The outer primaries are also broader and fresher at the tips. No greater coverts or tertials appear to have been replaced during the prealternate molt but note at least two replaced scapulars near the joint of the wing. Photo: Janet M. Ruth

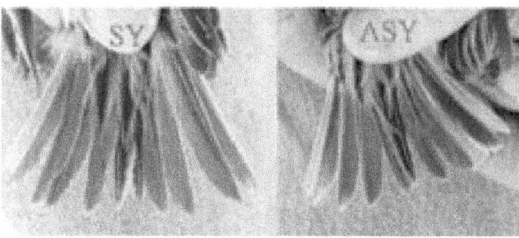

Figure 20. Shape and condition of the rectrices in Baird's Sparrows captured for banding in Montana in June. Note that the SY appears to have replaced the central rectrices during the preformative and/or prealternate molt and that the ASY has replaced the right central rectrix during the prealternate molt. Photos: Janet M. Ruth

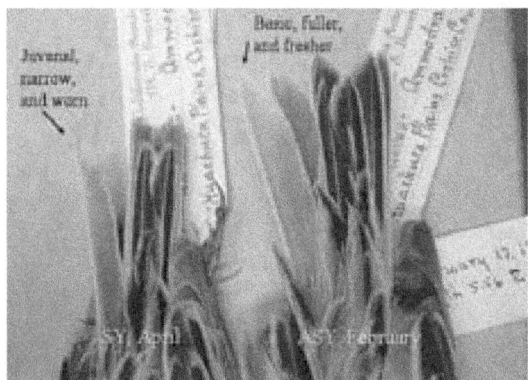 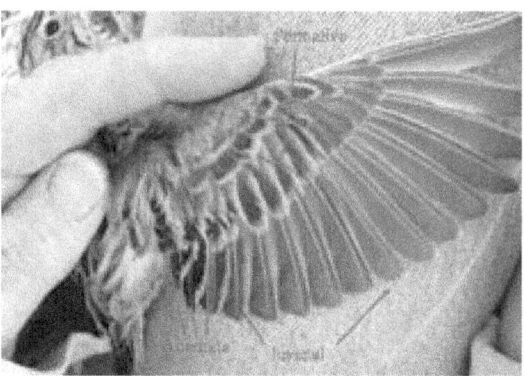

Figure 21. Shape and condition of the outer rectrices in SY and ASY Baird's Sparrows collected in Arizona. Some individuals show intermediate conditions that would be unreliable to use for aging. Note that the central rectrices appear to have been replaced during preformative and/or prealternate molts (see Figure 20). Photo: Peter Pyle

Figure 22. SY Baird's Sparrow in Montana in June. Biochemical signals can be obtained for this individual's natal site (juvenal secondaries and primaries), wintering site (alternate scapulars, tertials, and inner greater coverts), and possibly other molting sites (formative greater outer coverts). Photo: Janet M. Ruth

Chestnut-collared Longspur.

CHESTNUT-COLLARED LONGSPUR (*Calcarius ornatus*)

Molt.--In HY Chestnut-collared Longspurs, the preformative molt occurs on the breeding grounds from July - September and is partial (Figure 1D). Compared to the other three species treated here, this molt is less complete, typically including body feathers but no wing or tail feathers. In AHYs, the prebasic molt also occurs in July - September, on or near the breeding grounds, and it is complete. Thus, neither HY/SY nor AHY/ASY Chestnut-collared Longspurs will show molt limits in the wing at any time of the year (Figure 23). Pyle (1997a) indicates that some individuals may undergo a limited prealternate molt of head and breast feathers but a recent examination of specimens failed to detect any certain alternate feathers on spring and summer birds. The colorful black and chestnut feathers of males, developed during the preformative or prebasic molts, are tipped buff in fall and winter. This buff tipping then wears off by spring, unveiling the colorful "breeding" formative and basic plumage aspect. However, there may also be a few feathers replaced on some birds, and it would be important to recognize and sample these feathers to obtain a signal from winter grounds.

Age Determination.-- Condition of the wing coverts and amount of white edging to the inner primary coverts should also allow reliable aging of most individuals (Figures 23 and 24). Probably the most reliable method of aging Chestnut-collared Longspurs throughout the year is by the shape of the rectrices (Figure 25). Within each sex, AHY/ASYs will average brighter plumage than HY/SYs

(e.g., see Figure 23), especially in males during the breeding season. Unlike other species, the presence or absence of molt limits in the wing will not provide a clue to age.

Feather Sampling for Biochemical Analysis.-- Unlike in the other species treated here, most or all feathers will likely yield a signal from the breeding grounds. It will thus be of interest to collect feather samples from wintering grounds to determine breeding or molting localities. Some or all individuals may migrate away from their nesting territories to undergo the preformative or prebasic molt, and it is possible that this difference may be detectable. For HY/SYs, sampling from any of the wing or tail feathers should yield a natal signal, whereas a body feather will yield the location of the preformative molt, which may or may not occur exactly on or near the natal site. AHY/ASYs will likely have undergone the entire prebasic molt in one locality but it may not necessarily be on the natal site, and obtaining information about this locality through biochemical analysis would be of interest.

On the breeding grounds, it is important to look for any newer feathers that may yield a winter signal. These may include a few head or breast feathers replaced during the prealternate molt or, especially, adventitiously replaced wing or tail feathers. Look for these adventitiously replaced feathers among the tertials, wing coverts, rump feathers, and rectrices, feathers that often are lost during stressful interactions or while avoiding predators.

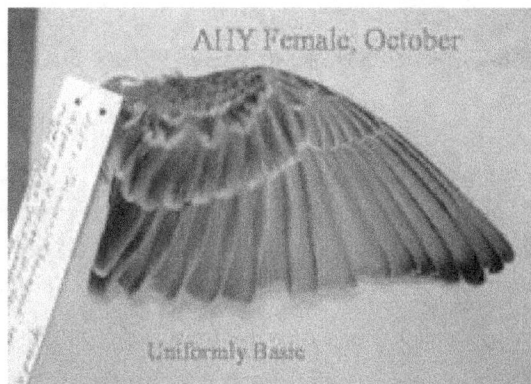

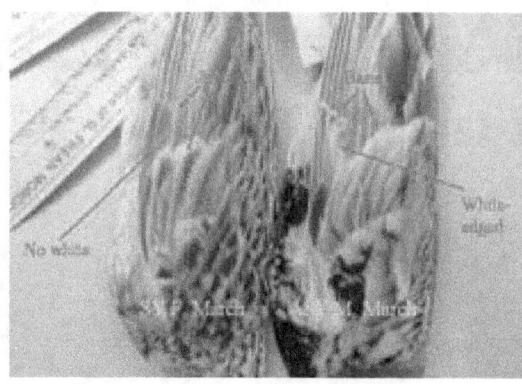

Figure 23. AHY female Chestnut-collared Longspur wing (collected in California) showing uniformly basic wing feathers. HY/SYs show uniformly juvenal wing feathers throughout the year; thus, molt limits in the wing cannot be used for aging Chestnut-collared Longspurs, unlike the other species treated here. Note the broad primary coverts and outer primary tips and the richly colored tertials and greater coverts which, for a female, combine to indicate an AHY/ASY (Figure 24). Photo: Peter Pyle

Figure 24. SY female and ASY male Chestnut-collared Longspurs collected on the wintering grounds in Arizona. Note the more worn wing coverts on the SY, and the lack of white on the inner primary coverts; within each sex, ASYs have more white than SYs (e.g., compare the SY female here with the AHY female in Figure 23). Photo: Peter Pyle

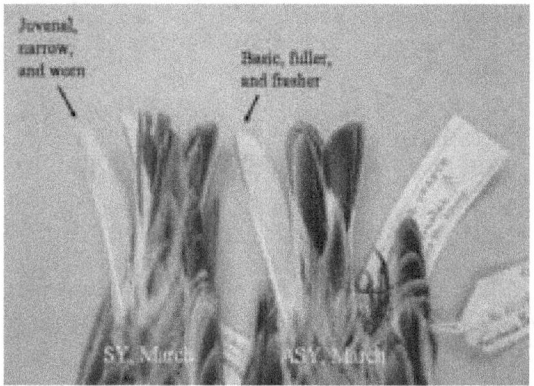

Figure 25. Shape and condition of the outer rectrices in Chestnut-collared Longspurs (collected in Texas). This criterion is reliable throughout the year. Photo: Peter Pyle

Literature Cited

Davis, S.K. 2003. Nesting ecology of mixed-grass prairie songbirds in southern Saskatchewan. Wilson Bulletin 115:119–130.

Davis, S.K. 2004. Area sensitivity in grassland passerines: effects of patch size, patch shape, and vegetation structure on bird abundance and occurrence in southern Saskatchewan. Auk 121:1130-1145.

Davis S.K., and S.G. Sealy. 1998. Nesting biology of the Baird's Sparrow in southwestern Manitoba. Wilson Bulletin 110:262–270.

DeSante, D.F. 1992. Monitoring avian productivity and survivorship (MAPS): a sharp, rather than blunt, tool for monitoring and assessing landbird populations. Pages 511-521 *in* D. R. McCullough and R.H. Barrett, editors. Wildlife 2001: populations. Elsevier Applied Science, London, England

DeSante, D.F. 1995. Suggestions for future directions for studies of marked migratory landbirds from the perspective of a practitioner in population management and conservation. Journal of Applied Statistics 22:949-965.

Dieni, J.S., and S.L. Jones. 2003. Grassland songbird nest site selection patterns in north central Montana. Wilson Bulletin 115:388-396.

Froehlich, D. 2003. Ageing North American landbirds by molt limits and plumage criteria. Slate Creek Press, Bolinas, California.

Howell, S.N.G., C. Corben, P. Pyle, and D. Rogers. 2003. The first basic problem: a review of molt and plumage homologies. Condor 105:635-653.

Humphrey, P.S., and K.C. Parkes. 1959. An approach to the study of molts and plumages. Auk 76:1-31.

Johnson, D.H., and L.D. Igl. 1997. Changes in breeding bird populations in North Dakota: 1997 to 1992-93. Auk 114:74-92.

Jones, S.L., and J.S. Dieni. 2007. The relationship between predation and nest concealment in mixed-grass prairie passerines: an analysis using program MARK. Studies in Avian Biology 34:117-123.

Jones, S.L., J.S. Dieni, M.T. Green, and P.J. Gouse. 2007. Annual return rates in breeding grassland songbirds. Wilson Bulletin of Ornithology 119:89-94.

Knopf, F.L. 1994. Avian assemblages on altered grasslands. Studies in Avian Biology 15:247–257.

Pérez, G., and K.A. Hobson. 2006. Isotopic evaluation of interrupted molt in northern breeding populations of the Loggerhead Shrike. Condor 108:877-886.

Peterjohn, B.G., and J.R. Sauer. 1999. Population status of North American grassland birds from the North American Breeding Bird Survey, 1966-1996. Studies in Avian Biology 19:27-44.

Pyle, P. 1997a. Identification guide to North American birds. Part 1. Slate Creek Press, Bolinas, California.

Pyle, P. 1997b. Molt limits in North American passerines. North American Bird Bander 22:49-90.

Smith, T. B., P.P. Marra, M.S. Webster, I. Lovette, L. Gibbs, and R.T. Holmes. 2003. A call for feather sampling. Auk 120:218-221.

Sauer, J.R., J.E. Hines, and J. Fallon. 2007. The North American Breeding Bird Survey, results and analysis 1966 - 2006. USGS Patuxent Wildlife Research Center, Laurel, Maryland. <http://www.mbr-pwrc.usgs.gov/bbs/> (7 April 2008).

Vickery, P.D. 1996. Grasshopper Sparrow (*Ammodramus savannarum*). *In* A. Poole and F. Gill, editors. The Birds of North America, No. 239. Academy of Natural Sciences, Philadelphia, Pennsylvania; The American Ornithologists' Union, Washington, D.C.

Appendix

Feather Collection Protocols for Analysis (Isotope and DNA)

For DNA analysis it is easiest to take two rectrices (tail feathers), which provides enough DNA to proceed with genetic analysis, although only one is needed for isotopic analysis. In general, we recommend taking a central rectrix from one side of the tail and an outer rectrix from the other side of the tail. This will keep the tail as "balanced" as possible while also preserving rectrices that are most likely to have been grown at different times of year or in different locations, thus resulting in more data from the individual based on isotopic analyses. For example, the central rectrix may have been grown on the breeding grounds followed by suspension for migration and replacement of the outer rectrix on the wintering grounds, or all rectrices may have developed on the breeding grounds and the central rectrix replaced again on the wintering grounds during a prealternate molt, resulting in signals from both breeding and a wintering grounds from the same individual. For isotopic analyses it is also useful, for the same reason, to take feathers or feather samples from other parts of the body. These might include juvenal feathers from nestlings; newer, alternate back feathers from breeding individuals, or samples from the bases of inner and outer primaries, which may have grown at different localities (see Pérez and Hobson 2006 for examples and methods). By knowing molt patterns and bird age it may be possible to get feather samples from three locations from a single individual.

1) To take a rectrix hold the tail feathers close to the base with your fingers and gently pull it out. Please take care not to touch the feather (quill) once you have pulled out the feather as this is where the DNA is tested. Feathers need to be pulled and not cut because: a) they will then grow back; b) the DNA is found within the skin cells at the base of the feather. For back feathers from nestlings, simply and gently pluck the feathers. Put feathers from each nestling in a separate envelope. For primaries it is best to take a section of barbs from the inner web of each sampled primary. Primaries are too hard to pull out, and taking a small (~ 1cm x 1 cm) section will allow the bird to continue flying without hindrance.

2) Insert the feather(s) into a coin envelope. Only use one envelope per individual; in some cases it might be advisable to use separate envelopes for separate feathers or feather generations from the same individual and to clearly mark which feathers are in each envelope.

3) Write the following information on the outside of the envelope. Use pencil or permanent ink (so it doesn't run on the feathers in case the sample gets wet). For nestlings, in the comments section or on the back, record the other band numbers of their siblings; we need to be able to sort out related individuals. Remarks should include where the feather was sampled and what generation (juvenal, formative, basic, alternate) the feather was believed to be.

Record:
    Species, Sex, Age (if known), Date, Location (including the state), and Band Number. Remarks: include what feather tract sampled; relationship to other samples, etc.

4) Store samples in a dry place, in a sealed plastic bag; any humidity or water can ruin the sample.